WEIRD CHRISTMAS
FESTIVE ODDITIES FROM AROUND THE WORLD
TRADITIONS

Copyright © 2023 by Michael Brown

All rights reserved. No part of this publication may be reproduced, distributed, or transmitted in any form or by any means, including photocopying, recording, or other electronic or mechanical methods, without the prior written permission of the publisher, except in the case of brief quotations embodied in critical reviews and certain other noncommercial uses permitted by copyright law.

First Edition, 2023

The views and opinions expressed in this book are those of the author(s) and do not necessarily reflect the official policy or position of the publisher. Names, characters, businesses, places, events, locales, and incidents are either the products of the author's imagination or used in a fictitious manner. Any resemblance to actual persons, living or dead, or actual events is purely coincidental.

INTRODUCTION

Welcome to a festive foray into the bizarre and unexpected corners of holiday celebrations with *"Weird Christmas Traditions: Festive Oddities from Around the World."* This book is not your typical Christmas story. Instead, it's an enchanting sleigh ride around the world, uncovering the most unusual and astonishing ways that different cultures embrace the holiday spirit.

From the sun-soaked beaches where Santas surf, to the icy landscapes where Christmas comes with a side of fermented birds, each chapter in this book is a window into the fascinating, sometimes inexplicable, but always entertaining traditions that define the season for people across the planet.

Prepare to be regaled with tales of Christmas monsters who keep naughty children in line, and to marvel at the curious dishes that grace the holiday tables in far-flung places. Delight in learning about the peculiar gifts exchanged—from practical jokes to tokens of love that defy convention. Laugh at the lighthearted games, gasp at the decoration disasters, and hum along to the strangest carols ever sung.

This book is a tribute to the wonderful weirdness of Christmas, a testament to humanity's creativity and a joyful reminder that, no matter how different our traditions may be, the essence of the holiday season is universal. So, grab a mug of your favorite holiday drink, settle into a cozy nook, and prepare to explore the quirkiest customs that make Christmas the most wonderfully weird time of the year.

WEIRD CHRISTMAS
FESTIVE ODDITIES FROM AROUND THE WORLD
TRADITIONS

MICHAEL BROWN

CONTENTS

Introduction — 3

1. Feasting Oddities — 7
2. Merry Monsters — 13
3. Tinsel Town Anomalies — 19
4. Gift-Giving Glitches — 25
5. Yuletide Games — 31
6. Decoration Disasters — 37
7. Carol Conundrums — 43
8. Santa's Wardrobe — 49
9. Nativity Narratives — 55
10. Unconventional Trees — 61
11. Holiday Transport Troubles — 67
12. The Great Christmas Comms — 73
13. The Economics of Yuletide — 79
14. Yule Laws and Legislation — 85
15. Polar Pranks — 91
16. Mistletoe Mishaps — 97
17. Santa School — 103
18. The Christmas Pickle — 109
19. Yuletide in Space — 115

DID YOU KNOW?

In Greenland's challenging climate, traditional foods are often as unique as they are practical. Another startling detail about Kiviak is that the birds are placed into the seal skin whole after a careful process, feathers and all. The seal skin is then sewn up and sealed with seal fat to keep out the air. Over the course of several months, the birds ferment in this natural container under a pile of stones, with the seal fat helping to prevent spoilage. When the Kiviak is finally opened, it's said that the aroma is pungent, and the taste is very intense, often described as cheesy with a hint of fishiness.

FEASTING ODDITIES

1. GREENLAND'S KIVIAK:

In a tradition not for the faint of heart, small birds called auks are fermented in a seal skin for months and eaten during Christmas in Greenland.

2. JAPAN'S CHRISTMAS CAKE:

Unlike traditional fruitcakes, Japanese Christmas is celebrated with a strawberry shortcake, adorned with whipped cream and fresh strawberries, symbolizing the country's love for all things kawaii (cute).

3. SWEDEN'S LUTEFISK:

This gelatinous fish dish made from aged stockfish and lye is a Scandinavian Christmas staple, with a pungent aroma that's as strong as its flavor.

4. ITALY'S FEAST OF THE SEVEN FISHES:

Italians celebrate Christmas Eve with a grand meal consisting of seven different seafood dishes, symbolizing the seven sacraments.

5. SOUTH AFRICA'S FRIED CATERPILLARS:

A treat for the brave, mopane caterpillars are a protein-rich snack typically enjoyed during the Christmas season.

6. UKRAINE'S KUTYA:

A sweet porridge made of wheatberries, poppy seeds, and honey, Kutya is a traditional Christmas Eve dish that's shared to ensure good fortune.

7. GERMANY'S STOLLEN:

A dense bread filled with dried fruit, marzipan, and dusted with powdered sugar, resembling a baby Jesus swaddled in clothes.

8. PORTUGAL'S CONSOADA:

A Christmas Eve feast that involves boiled codfish with cabbage and potatoes, followed by a variety of sweet pastries.

9. MEXICO'S BACALAO:

A traditional Christmas Eve dish, bacalao is salted codfish cooked with tomatoes, onions, olives, and capers.

10. ICELAND'S HANGIKJÖT:

Smoked lamb is a Christmas specialty in Iceland, often accompanied by béchamel sauce and boiled potatoes.

11. PHILIPPINES' PUTO BUMBONG:

After the Simbang Gabi (night mass), Filipinos enjoy this purple rice delicacy, cooked in bamboo tubes and served with butter, sugar, and grated coconut.

12. ENGLAND'S MINCE PIES:

Once filled with meat, now these small pies are packed with a mixture of dried fruits and spices called 'mincemeat', and are a Christmas dessert staple.

13. AUSTRALIA'S BBQ CHRISTMAS:

With December being summertime in Australia, a Christmas barbecue often replaces the hot roast dinner, featuring seafood and traditional meats.

14. CZECH REPUBLIC'S FRIED CARP:

Carp is the Christmas Eve meal of choice, often bought live and kept in bathtubs before being fried and served.

15. SLOVAKIA'S LOKSA:

A Christmas bread made from potato dough and filled with a mixture of poppy seeds and honey, often eaten after the Christmas Eve fast.

16. FRANCE'S RÉVEILLON:

A long dinner held on Christmas Eve, featuring dishes like oysters, foie gras, and a variety of cheeses, followed by a Bûche de Noël dessert.

17. NEW ZEALAND'S PAVLOVA:

A meringue-based dessert named after the Russian ballerina Anna Pavlova, topped with whipped cream and fresh fruits, and argued over with Australia about its origin.

18. CATALONIA'S TURRÓN:

A nougat made from almonds and honey, often consumed during Christmas in Catalonia, with a variety of flavors ranging from chocolate to fruit.

19. FINLAND'S JOULUPÖYTÄ:

The Finnish Christmas table offers an array of dishes, but the standout is the Christmas ham, slow-cooked and glazed with mustard.

20. PERU'S PANETTONE:

Known locally as 'Panetón', this sweet bread filled with candied fruits is a fusion of Italian and Peruvian traditions, enjoyed with hot chocolate.

21. CANADA'S TOURTIÈRE:

In Quebec, families enjoy this meat pie made with minced pork, beef, or game meat, spiced with cloves, cinnamon, and nutmeg, during Réveillon.

22. SPAIN'S SEAFOOD:

While varied across regions, Spaniards often indulge in seafood during Christmas, from prawns and lobsters to clams and mussels.

23. AUSTRIA'S CHRISTMAS GOOSE:

A succulent goose often replaces turkey on the Christmas table in Austria, served with red cabbage and dumplings.

24. RUSSIA'S OLIVIER SALAD:

A Russian holiday feast is incomplete without this salad made with potatoes, vegetables, eggs, meat, and mayonnaise, named after a French chef.

25. BRAZIL'S CHESTER:

A type of chicken that's been selectively bred to have more breast meat, Chester is often roasted whole and is a Christmas favorite in Brazil.

DID YOU KNOW?

In Iceland, the Yule Lad named "Window Peeper" is a curious character who sneaks around to peer through windows in search of toys to steal. His approach is both creepy and comical, as he's often depicted with wide, eager eyes, pressing his nose against the glass, scouting for his next trinket to swipe.

MERRY MONSTERS

1. ICELAND'S YULE LADS:

Thirteen mischievous trolls visit Icelandic children in the 13 days leading to Christmas, each with his own peculiar habit, like slamming doors or stealing milk.

2. AUSTRIA'S KRAMPUS:

The antithesis of Saint Nicholas, Krampus is a horned figure who punishes naughty children. December 5th, known as Krampusnacht, sees men dressing up as the creature, roaming the streets and scaring onlookers.

3. GERMANY'S BELSNICKEL:

This fur-clad figure, often carrying a switch, visits homes to determine if children have been behaving, dispensing candy or gentle whacks as needed.

4. FRANCE'S PÈRE FOUETTARD:

Accompanying St. Nicholas in parts of France, this bogeyman figure doles out lumps of coal or floggings to misbehaving children while St. Nick gives gifts.

5. NORWAY'S JULEBUKK:

A Christmas goat figure that is based on the Norse god Thor's goats. People dress up in goat masks and costumes, visiting houses for treats.

6. ITALY'S LA BEFANA:

A friendly witch who delivers gifts to children on Epiphany Eve (January 5th), much like Santa Claus, but also sweeps the floor before she leaves.

7. WALES' MARI LWYD:

A horse's skull adorned with ribbons and bells, carried on a pole and draped with a cloth. It's taken door-to-door, where the Mari Lwyd and householders exchange playful insults in verse.

8. NETHERLANDS' ZWARTE PIET:

St. Nicholas's helper, portrayed in colorful pantaloons and with a blackened face, who distributes sweets and small gifts to children.

9. CATALONIA'S TIÓ DE NADAL:

A smiling log that 'poops' out presents for children when they beat it with sticks while singing traditional songs.

10. FINLAND'S NUUTTIPUKKI:

A goat-like figure that goes from house to house demanding leftover food after Christmas, related to the tradition of St. Knut's Day.

11. PORTUGAL'S CONSODA:

An empty place is set at the Christmas table for the alminhas a penar ("souls of the dead"), to bring them luck in the afterlife.

12. SLOVENIA'S PARKELJ:

A Krampus-like figure that accompanies St. Nicholas, covered in dark fur and wearing a horned mask to scare those who aren't well-behaved.

13. UKRAINE'S KOLYADKY:

Not monsters but mischievous carolers who dress in costumes, often as demonic figures, to perform traditional songs in exchange for treats.

14. SWITZERLAND'S SCHMUTZLI:

A companion of Samichlaus (Swiss St. Nicholas), Schmutzli carries a sack of ashes for naughty children and a basket of treats for the good ones.

15. CZECH REPUBLIC'S ČERT:

A devilish figure that appears alongside St. Nicholas and an angel, the trio visiting children to judge their behavior over the past year.

16. HUNGARY'S KRAMPUSZ:

Accompanying St. Nicholas, Krampusz scares children into good behavior with his devilish appearance and rattling chains.

17. BELGIUM'S HANS TRAPP:

An anti-Santa who, legend has it, was excommunicated and turned into a scarecrow. He now accompanies St. Nicholas to frighten children into being good.

18. GREECE'S KALLIKANTZAROI:

Goblins that emerge during the 12 days of Christmas, causing mischief like souring milk and extinguishing fires unless deterred by protective marks or colanders.

19. SERBIA'S TUCINDAN:

A pre-Christmas day when an oak branch is cut and brought into the home to burn, believed to protect the family from evil spirits.

20. BASQUE COUNTRY'S OLENTZERO:

A giant who descends from the mountains to bring gifts to children, but he also has a darker side, as he is said to have been a pagan enforcer before his conversion to Christianity.

21. SCOTLAND'S FIRST FOOTER:

After midnight on Hogmanay (New Year's Eve), the first person to cross a home's threshold should carry a lump of coal for good luck, but folklore suggests a dark-haired man is the most auspicious.

22. SARDINIA'S SU NENNIRI:

An old lady puppet that is carried around villages to scare children, reminding them to be good or face being taken away in her sack.

23. ALBANIA'S KALLIKANTZAROI:

Similar to the Greek tradition, these Christmas creatures come up from the underworld to play tricks on humans until they are sent back by the ringing of church bells for Epiphany.

24. BRAZIL'S HEADLESS MULE:

A cursed character from folklore that appears on Christmas as a fire-spewing mule, a figure used to instill fear and good behavior in children.

25. IRELAND'S THE WREN BOYS:

On St. Stephen's Day, December 26th, people dress up in old clothes, straw hats, and masks, going door-to-door singing, dancing, and playing music, originally to scare away evil spirits for the new year.

DID YOU KNOW?

Egypt's Christmas celebrations take a unique turn with camel parades, where the traditional sleigh and reindeer are replaced by "ships of the desert." Decked out in bright fabrics and ornaments, these camels traverse the streets, bringing a local twist to holiday festivities. This fusion of global and native traditions captivates both young and old, creating a spectacle of joy and cultural pride. It's a holiday enchantment rooted in Egyptian sands, showcasing a different but equally magical facet of the Christmas cheer.

TINSEL TOWN ANOMALIES

1. CAMEL PARADE IN EGYPT:

Reflecting the desert landscape, Christmas parades often feature camels decked in festive attire, a unique twist on the traditional reindeer-led sleigh.

2. SURFING SANTAS IN AUSTRALIA:

Every Christmas, hundreds of Santas grab their surfboards and hit the waves in Bondi Beach, creating a spectacular sea of red and white amidst the blue waves.

3. KRAMPUS RUN IN AUSTRIA:

Men dressed as Krampus, a horned Christmas demon, run through the streets, chasing and playfully whipping spectators, in a centuries-old tradition meant to scare away evil spirits.

4. ROLLERBLADING TO MASS IN VENEZUELA:

In Caracas, it's a Christmas Eve tradition to rollerblade to early morning mass, with streets closed to cars to ensure safety for the blading faithful.

5. GÄVLE GOAT IN SWEDEN:

Since 1966, a giant straw goat is erected in Gävle for Christmas, which more often than not becomes a target for arson, adding an unusual twist to festive decorations.

6. CAGANER FIGURES IN CATALONIA:

Nativity scenes in Catalonia include the Caganer, a figure depicted in the act of defecation, symbolizing fertility and bringing good luck by "fertilizing" the earth.

7. CHRISTMAS WITCH IN ITALY:

La Befana, the friendly witch of Italian folklore, delivers gifts to children on Epiphany Eve, riding a broomstick rather than a sleigh.

8. RADISH CARVING FESTIVAL IN MEXICO:

Oaxaca hosts 'Noche de los Rábanos', where artisans carve intricate scenes from radishes, including nativity scenes and traditional Mexican motifs.

9. BANANA TREE CHRISTMAS IN INDIA:

Some Christians in India decorate banana or mango trees instead of traditional pines, adapting the festive tradition to local flora.

10. SPIDER WEBS IN UKRAINE:

Ukrainian Christmas trees often sparkle with spider web ornaments, a tradition inspired by a folktale where spiders wove webs that turned into gold and silver strands.

11. SHOE TOSSING IN THE CZECH REPUBLIC:

Single Czech women toss a shoe over their shoulder at Christmas; if it lands with the toe pointing towards the door, it means marriage is on the horizon.

12. YULE CAT IN ICELAND:

The Jólakötturinn or Yule Cat is said to roam the snowy countryside, and legend has it that those who don't receive new clothes before Christmas Eve will be devoured by this mythical beast.

13. KENTUCKY FRIED CHRISTMAS IN JAPAN:

A quirky marketing campaign in the 1970s turned KFC into a Christmas tradition in Japan, with families enjoying buckets of fried chicken to celebrate the festive season.

14. NIGHT OF THE RADISHES IN MEXICO:

A quirky tradition held on December 23rd where artisans create elaborate scenes carved from radishes, including nativity scenes and other festive motifs.

15. GIANT LANTERN FESTIVAL IN THE PHILIPPINES:

The city of San Fernando holds a lantern festival where giant lanterns, some with thousands of spinning lights, illuminate the night in a dazzling display of Christmas spirit.

16. MONKEY BUFFET IN THAILAND:

In Lopburi, a banquet for monkeys is laid out on tables during the festival, as these revered animals are treated to a feast of fruits and vegetables in a unique celebration.

17. 'THE BURNING OF THE DEVIL' IN GUATEMALA:

Guatemalans sweep out their houses, collecting trash and unwanted items to burn in a heap as a symbolic devil, purifying their homes for Christmas.

18. SWIMMING SANTAS IN DENMARK:

In Copenhagen, a crowd of Santas brave the icy waters for a Christmas swim, turning heads with their festive, albeit chilly, dip.

19. CHRISTMAS LOG IN CATALONIA:

The 'Caga Tió', or pooping log, is a wooden log that "poops" out presents for children when hit with sticks, combining tradition with a bit of humor.

20. FIREWORKS CHRISTMAS IN MALTA:

Christmas in Malta is welcomed with a bang, as the night skies are lit up with fireworks, a blend of festive joy and the island's love for pyrotechnics.

21. 'LITTLE CHRISTMAS' WOMEN'S HOLIDAY IN IRELAND:

On January 6th, women rest and celebrate while men take on the household duties, an appreciation for the women's hard work over the festive season.

22. 'CHRISTMAS PICKLE' IN THE UNITED STATES:

A pickle-shaped ornament is hidden on the Christmas tree, with the finder usually receiving a reward or good fortune for the coming year.

23. ICE SKATING MASS IN THE NETHERLANDS:

If the canals freeze over in winter, it's a tradition for some Dutch to ice skate to Christmas Day mass.

24. 'HIDE THE BROOM' IN NORWAY:

Norwegians hide all their brooms before bedtime on Christmas Eve to prevent them from being stolen by witches and evil spirits.

25. PORRIDGE WITH AN ALMOND IN SWEDEN:

During Christmas, Swedes eat rice porridge with one hidden almond; the finder is expected to get married within the year, adding a touch of destiny to the feast.

DID YOU KNOW?

In Iceland, the quirky 'jólabanani' or Christmas Banana tradition brings humor to the holidays. Loved ones playfully hide bananas in shoes or stockings, offering a whimsical and healthful twist to the usual sweet treats. This light-hearted custom adds an element of surprise and delight to Icelandic Christmas, showcasing the country's unique take on festive gifting.

GIFT-GIVING GLITCHES

1. **SECRET BANANA IN ICELAND:**

   In Iceland, friends and families sometimes sneak a 'jólabanani', or Christmas Banana, into each other's shoes or stockings, as a humorous, healthy alternative to candy.

2. **SHOEBOX DONATIONS IN THE UK:**

   Millions fill shoeboxes with gifts and essentials for Operation Christmas Child, sending them to children in need worldwide, a tradition of giving that goes beyond the usual gift exchanges.

3. **CONSOLATION PRIZE IN SPAIN:**

   During 'El Gordo', a massive Christmas lottery, those who don't win the jackpot often buy each other 'pedreas' or consolation prizes, turning loss into a quirky gift exchange.

4. **SPIDER ORNAMENTS IN UKRAINE:**

   Inspired by a folktale, Ukrainians gift each other spider-shaped decorations believed to bring good luck and fortune, weaving a web of happiness for the receiver.

5. COAL FOR THE NAUGHTY IN ITALY:

La Befana, the Italian Christmas witch, leaves a lump of coal for naughty children, though it's often sweet, edible coal, turning naughtiness into a treat.

6. GARLIC BULBS IN PORTUGAL:

A Portuguese tradition includes gifting garlic bulbs, a symbol of health and prosperity, ensuring the recipient remains strong and hearty throughout the coming year.

7. BOOK FLOOD IN ICELAND:

Jólabókaflóð, or the Christmas Book Flood, is a tradition where people gift each other books to read on Christmas Eve, fostering a nation of literary enthusiasts.

8. WILDFLOWER SEEDS IN THE NETHERLANDS:

In the spirit of renewal, some Dutch gift wildflower seeds, encouraging friends and family to sow beauty for the spring, a symbolic gesture of growth and new beginnings.

9. RED UNDERWEAR IN ITALY:

In Italy, it's customary to gift red underwear on New Year's Eve, a tradition thought to bring good luck and joy to the recipient for the year ahead.

10. POTATO PRESENT IN GERMANY:

Some German families hide a potato in the Christmas tree, and the lucky finder receives a small, additional present, making for a 'rooting' good time.

GIFT-GIVING GLITCHES

11. ALUMINUM FOIL BALL IN NORWAY:

Norwegians wrap up leftover Christmas Eve chocolate in aluminum foil, forming a ball that gets larger each year, a sweet and sustainable tradition passed down.

12. EGGBEATER IN HUNGARY:

In Hungary, an eggbeater is sometimes given, symbolizing the start of the holiday baking season, whisking up sentiments of warmth and family traditions.

13. MYSTERY GIFT AUCTIONS IN CANADA:

'White Elephant' gift exchanges where participants bid on wrapped mystery gifts often result in hilarious unveilings, from quirky novelties to gag gifts.

14. FRIENDSHIP POUCH IN JAPAN:

It's a Japanese tradition to give small pouches filled with tokens or notes of appreciation, symbolizing friendship and gratitude during the festive season.

15. SILLY SOCKS IN AUSTRALIA:

Australians exchange colorful and often ridiculous novelty socks, bringing a touch of humor and warmth to the holiday season.

16. GAG GIFTS IN THE USA:

Americans love to exchange humorous gag gifts, often at office parties or family gatherings, sparking laughter and light-heartedness.

17. WISH LANTERNS IN CHINA:

During the Lantern Festival, which coincides with the Lunar New Year close to Christmas, people gift lanterns to make a wish for the coming year.

18. CHRISTMAS GOATS IN FINLAND:

Small straw goats are a common gift, paying homage to the Yule Goat tradition, and are thought to bring good cheer.

19. CACTUS PLANTS IN MEXICO:

Reflecting the desert landscape, it's not uncommon to gift a decorated Christmas Cactus instead of a potted fir, adding a local touch to the festive decor.

20. LOVE SPOONS IN WALES:

Intricately carved wooden spoons are gifted as a token of affection, a Welsh tradition that symbolizes love and companionship.

21. PUZZLE PIECES IN BELGIUM:

Belgians sometimes gift a single puzzle piece, starting a family puzzle that everyone contributes to and completes together during the holiday season.

22. BREAD DOLLS IN GREECE:

In Greece, it's a tradition to gift 'Christopsomo', a Christmas bread with a coin or doll baked inside, bringing good fortune to the finder.

GIFT-GIVING GLITCHES

23. PERSONALIZED POEMS IN ICELAND:

Along with the book flood, some Icelanders write personal poems for their loved ones, crafting heartfelt verses that are often more treasured than store-bought gifts.

24. MISMATCHED MITTENS IN CANADA:

In some parts of Canada, gifting a single mitten with a promise to deliver the match later is a quirky way to ensure a second meeting.

25. LOTTERY TICKETS IN SPAIN:

It's customary to gift lottery tickets for 'El Gordo', the big Christmas lottery, sharing the dream of holiday fortune and perhaps, a life-changing win.

DID YOU KNOW?

In Italy, Christmas gifting is entwined with destiny through the 'Urn of Fate'. It's a heartwarming tradition where family members draw surprise gifts from a deep, decorative bowl, each present a secret until chosen. This time-honored ritual adds suspense and excitement to the holiday, as the contents of the urn hold anonymous tokens of affection. Everyone, from the youngest to the eldest, partakes in the anticipation, embracing the serendipity of the season and the joyous bonds it celebrates.

YULETIDE GAMES

1. ITALY'S 'URN OF FATE':

Italian families pick gifts from the 'Urn of Fate', a lucky dip of presents, ensuring everyone gets a surprise, adding an element of destiny to gift-giving.

2. CATALONIA'S CAGA TIÓ:

In Catalonia, children beat a log adorned with a smiling face, the 'Caga Tió', which 'poops out' treats and gifts when hit with sticks while singing a traditional song.

3. ICELAND'S JÓLABÓKAFLÓÐ:

Iceland celebrates Christmas Eve with the 'Book Flood' where people exchange books and spend the evening reading, making literature a central part of their festive fun.

4. JAPAN'S CHRISTMAS CAKE GAME:

Japanese families play a game where they decorate a plain sponge cake together, and the quirkiest decoration wins, adding a sweet competitive spirit to the holiday.

5. GERMANY'S 'HIDE THE PICKLE':

A pickle-shaped ornament is hidden within the Christmas tree, and the first child to find it on Christmas morning receives an extra gift.

6. NORWAY'S ALMOND IN RICE PUDDING:

Norwegians hide a whole almond in rice pudding, and whoever finds it in their serving wins a small prize, often a marzipan pig.

7. WALES' MARI LWYD:

A peculiar Welsh tradition where people parade with a horse skull on a pole, going door-to-door exchanging playful verses for food and drink.

8. UKRAINE'S SPIDER WEB HUNT:

Ukrainian children search for the hidden artificial spider web in the Christmas tree; finding it is believed to bring good luck.

9. PHILIPPINES' 'MONITO MONITA':

A form of secret Santa known as 'Monito Monita', where Filipinos exchange themed gifts leading up to Christmas, each day with a different fun category.

10. VENEZUELA'S ROLLER-SKATING TO MASS:

In Caracas, it's a quirky tradition to roller-skate to Christmas mass, with streets closed to cars to safely accommodate the festive skaters.

11. SWEDISH 'FIND THE GUEST':

A game where a small guest figurine is hidden in the Christmas porridge, and whoever finds it in their serving is expected to host the next holiday gathering.

12. BELGIUM'S 'SNEAKY PETE':

Children play 'Sneaky Pete', trying to place a paper Santa hat on unsuspecting family members' heads without them noticing.

13. FINLAND'S CHRISTMAS SAUNA SPIRITS:

Finns believe spirits visit the sauna on Christmas Eve, so they leave it empty and visit themselves to relax and play gentle steam-based games.

14. GREENLAND'S 'KICK THE CAN':

A simple game where families kick a can filled with small gifts and candies, spreading them across the floor for children to collect.

15. BRAZIL'S 'AMIGO SECRETO':

Similar to secret Santa, Brazilians play 'Amigo Secreto', where friends and family draw names to exchange gifts, often accompanied by a playful poem about the recipient.

16. FRENCH 'PÈRE FOUETTARD' QUIZ:

In France, children play a quiz game where they must answer questions correctly or face a mock scolding from Père Fouettard, Santa's disciplinarian companion.

17. SCOTTISH 'FIRST FOOTER' CHALLENGE:

The first person to enter a home after midnight on Christmas is the 'First Footer' and is said to bring luck. Families often playfully compete to be the first.

18. AUSTRIAN 'KRAMPUS RUN':

In a wilder tradition, Austrians participate in 'Krampus Runs', where people dress as the fearsome Krampus and chase others through the streets.

19. DUTCH 'SINTERKLAAS' BINGO:

The Dutch play a form of bingo on St. Nicholas Day with gifts and riddles, adding a cultural twist to the holiday fun.

20. MEXICAN 'PIÑATA STAR':

Mexican children take turns being blindfolded and hitting a star-shaped piñata, eagerly collecting the fallen treats, a vibrant part of any Christmas gathering.

21. CANADIAN 'GUESS THE GIFT':

Before opening presents, Canadian families guess the contents based on the shape and sound of the package, with correct guessers earning the privilege to open first.

22. RUSSIAN 'FORTUNE-TELLING':

Russian Christmas involves games of fortune-telling, where various objects are placed under pillows, and the one you find predicts your fate for the coming year.

23. INDIAN 'CHRISTMAS ANTAKSHARI':

Combining Christmas carols with the traditional game of 'Antakshari', where teams sing songs starting with the last letter of the previous song.

24. CZECH 'SHOE TOSS':

Czech singles throw a shoe over their shoulder towards the door; if the toe points towards the door when it lands, marriage is said to be on the horizon.

25. AUSTRALIAN 'BEACH CRICKET':

An Aussie twist to Christmas games, families and friends hit the beach for a friendly game of cricket, celebrating the holiday with sport and sun.

DID YOU KNOW?

In Venezuela, a whimsical tradition turns Christmas trees into glittering masterpieces with the addition of artificial spider webs. This custom has its roots in a charming folk tale where benevolent spiders wove their webs around a tree, which miraculously transformed into glistening gold and silver strands with the first light of Christmas Day. This festive practice captures the enchantment of the holiday, merging the natural wonder of spider silk with the magical aura of Christmas, creating a visual spectacle that delights and surprises in the spirit of the season.

DECORATION DISASTERS

1. VENEZUELA'S SPIDER WEBS:

Venezuelans decorate their trees with fake spider webs, a tradition stemming from a folk tale where spiders covered a tree in webs which turned to gold and silver on Christmas morning.

2. UKRAINE'S LUCKY SPIDER:

In Ukraine, finding a real spider or a web on your Christmas tree is considered good luck, inspiring a tradition of spider ornaments known as "pavuchky".

3. NORWAY'S HIDDEN BROOMS:

Norwegians hide all their brooms on Christmas Eve to prevent them from being stolen by witches and evil spirits, a quirky protective tradition.

4. GERMANY'S PICKLE ORNAMENT:

The last ornament to be hung on the tree is a glass pickle, hidden among the branches. The first child to find it on Christmas morning gets a special treat.

5. ICELAND'S YULE CAT ORNAMENT:

To appease the Yule Cat, a monstrous feline that eats those without new clothes, Icelanders hang cat ornaments and gift clothing to avoid its 'wrath'.

6. SOUTH AFRICAN FLOWER CHRISTMAS TREES:

Instead of traditional pine trees, South Africans often decorate their homes with native flowers, leading to vibrant, colorful "trees".

7. ITALIAN WITCH BEFANA:

In Italy, the Christmas witch Befana is said to sweep away the problems of the year, inspiring broomstick ornaments and decorations.

8. JAPANESE ORIGAMI ORNAMENTS:

In Japan, families often fold origami swans and stars to decorate their Christmas trees, a fusion of traditional craft and western celebration.

9. BRAZIL'S TROPICAL TREE:

In Brazil, Christmas trees are sometimes adorned with cotton to simulate snow, a humorous nod to the tropical climate.

10. CZECH CHAINS:

Czechs create chains made from apples, nuts, and sweets which often break under their weight, leading to amusing decoration mishaps.

11. DUTCH WOODEN SHOES:

In the Netherlands, wooden shoes are filled with hay for Santa's horse and often end up as a humorous, oversized tree ornament.

12. MEXICAN RADISH NIGHT:

A quirky tradition in Oaxaca, Mexico, involves carving radishes into intricate scenes for Christmas, leading to a festive night known as "Noche de los Rábanos".

13. AUSTRALIAN 'SURFING SANTAS':

Australians place figures of Santa on a surfboard among their Christmas decor, a comical nod to their warm holiday season.

14. CANADIAN MAPLE LEAF WREATHS:

Canadians often use maple leaves in their Christmas wreaths, which have a tendency to crumble indoors, leaving a trail of the national symbol on the floor.

15. BRITISH 'CRACKER' MISHAPS:

In the UK, Christmas wouldn't be complete without crackers, which often malfunction, either not popping or exploding too vigorously, adding to the fun.

16. AMERICAN TINSEL TANGLES:

In the United States, pets and children often get tangled in the silver strands of tinsel, creating a humorous holiday hazard.

17. NEW ZEALAND'S POHUTUKAWA:

New Zealanders use the red-blossomed Pohutukawa tree as a Christmas symbol, which often sheds its flowers onto the holiday spread.

18. SWEDISH STRAW GOATS:

The Gävle Goat, a giant straw goat in Sweden, has an odd tradition of frequently being vandalized or burned down, despite being a beloved decoration.

19. FINNISH SAUNA ELVES:

In Finland, sauna 'elf' figurines are a common decoration, but they sometimes 'melt' in the heat, leading to humorous elf puddles.

20. GREEK BOAT DECORATIONS:

In Greece, boats are decorated instead of trees. However, cats often see these as a great place to nap, leading to the occasional capsized vessel.

21. POLISH GLASS ORNAMENTS:

Poland is famous for its intricate glass ornaments, but the fragility leads to annual stories of decoration disasters involving shattered heirlooms.

22. SLOVAKIAN WATERLOGGED CARP:

In Slovakia, a live carp is brought into the home and kept in the bathtub before Christmas dinner, often leading to slippery situations.

23. SPANISH 'CAGANER' FIGURINES:

In Catalonia, 'caganer' figures of people defecating are hidden in nativity scenes, a humorous tradition that adds a human touch to the divine story.

24. BELGIAN BEER BOTTLE TREES:

Some Belgians create Christmas trees from empty beer bottles, which occasionally collapse under their own weight, spilling a festive clatter.

25. RUSSIAN 'GRANDFATHER FROST' DOLLS:

Russian 'Grandfather Frost' is depicted in matryoshka dolls, which sometimes get stuck one inside the other, turning the unpacking into a laughable struggle.

DID YOU KNOW?

In the chill of Iceland's winter, the 'Yule Cat' song recounts a folklore giant cat, prowling the snowy landscape, preying on those not gifted with new attire for Christmas. This eerie tune serves both as a cautionary tale and an incentive, compelling children to toil diligently, thereby earning their new garments to elude the Yule Cat's appetite. The melody weaves a sense of urgency and tradition, as families gather to ensure no one is left vulnerable to the mythical feline's feast.

CAROL CONUNDRUMS

1. ICELAND'S 'YULE CAT' SONG:

A peculiar carol about a giant cat that eats those without new clothes, urging children to work hard and wear their finest to avoid being the Yule Cat's dinner.

2. WALES' MARI LWYD:

This carol accompanies a folk custom involving a horse's skull on a stick, draped in cloth, being paraded through town, challenging residents to a battle of rhyming insults in song.

3. AUSTRIA'S 'SILENT NIGHT' ORIGINS:

Penned during a time when the church organ was broken, this now-famous carol was originally played with a guitar, showcasing a humble beginning for a timeless tune.

4. UKRAINE'S 'SHCHEDRYK' (CAROL OF THE BELLS):

Initially a song celebrating the New Year, it was adapted into a Christmas carol telling the story of a swallow heralding good fortune.

5. SPAIN'S 'FUM, FUM, FUM':

A lively carol emphasizing the sound of the strumming guitar, it reflects the joy and festivity of the season with a distinctly Spanish rhythm and onomatopoeia.

6. NORWAY'S 'MUSEVISA' (THE MOUSE SONG):

A whimsical carol about a family of mice preparing for Christmas, avoiding the cat, and reveling in holiday cheese, showing the lighter side of the season.

7. GREEK 'KALANDA' (CHRISTMAS CAROLS):

These carols are often accompanied by triangles and sometimes humorous threats if the household doesn't offer treats or money, showcasing a cheeky aspect of Greek Christmas.

8. ITALIAN 'LA BEFANA' SONG:

This tune accompanies the tale of the Christmas witch, Befana, who delivers gifts to children, and is an unusual counterpart to more traditional carols.

9. FRENCH 'PETIT PAPA NOËL':

A beloved song where a child pleads with Santa for presents, it humorously addresses the anxieties kids have about being forgotten by Papa Noël.

10. SWEDISH 'NÄR JULDAGSMORGON GLIMMAR':

Sung early on Christmas morning, this carol has been humorously altered by children over the years, adding nonsensical verses much to adults' chagrin.

11. PORTUGUESE 'A TODOS UM BOM NATAL':

A carol that wishes everyone a good Christmas, often sung out of tune by enthusiastic children in school performances, much to their parents' amusement.

12. POLISH 'DZISIAJ W BETLEJEM':

This lively carol is known for its fast pace, which often leads to singers tripping over the words, resulting in humorous renditions during caroling.

13. DUTCH 'DE HERDERTJES LAGEN BIJ NACHTE':

Telling the story of shepherds at night, it's often sung out of key by merry Dutch revelers, adding a charmingly offbeat sound to the holidays.

14. CANADIAN 'HURON CAROL':

Canada's oldest Christmas song, originally written in the Huron language, it has humorous modern interpretations as singers attempt the ancient language.

15. BELGIAN 'KLING KLOKJE KLINGELINGELING':

A carol about bells ringing, often sung by children who add extra 'klingelings' for comedic effect, extending the song much longer than intended.

16. AUSTRALIAN 'SIX WHITE BOOMERS':

A quirky carol about Santa using kangaroos instead of reindeer in Australia, often resulting in boisterous 'booming' choruses from amused singers.

17. ENGLISH 'I SAW THREE SHIPS':

The mystery of how the ships could come to Bethlehem, a landlocked area, has inspired many humorous theories and whimsical performances.

18. AMERICAN 'GRANDMA GOT RUN OVER BY A REINDEER':

A novelty carol that has become a humorous reminder to watch out for reindeer, often eliciting laughter and eye-rolls in equal measure.

19. SCOTTISH 'AULD LANG SYNE':

Traditionally sung at New Year's but also at Christmas, the Scots dialect often leads to mumbled verses and enthusiastic but confused choruses.

20. FILIPINO 'ANG PASKO AY SUMAPIT':

This carol's upbeat tempo and Tagalog lyrics can result in lighthearted mistakes and laughter when non-speakers join in the singing.

21. NEW ZEALAND 'TE HARINUI':

Notable for its incorporation of Maori language, this carol often leads to playful but respectful attempts at pronunciation by New Zealanders of all backgrounds.

22. MEXICAN 'LOS PECES EN EL RÍO':

This carol, describing fishes in the river drinking and drinking as they witness the birth of Jesus, often amuses with its peculiar imagery.

23. BRAZILIAN 'BOAS FESTAS':

This carol, wishing 'good holidays,' often includes humorous improvisations by Brazilians, who add local slang and jokes into the verses.

24. RUSSIAN 'TWAS THE NIGHT BEFORE CHRISTMAS':

Not to be confused with the poem, this Russian carol is a humorous narrative often dramatized with over-the-top performances during caroling.

25. SOUTH AFRICAN 'COME COLOURS RISE':

This carol, sung in various South African languages, can lead to a vibrant mix of harmonies, languages, and the occasional humorous misstep in lyrics.

DID YOU KNOW?

In Japan, the iconic Santa Claus is sometimes reimagined as a noble samurai, clad in traditional armor. This Samurai Santa merges Western and Eastern traditions, embodying the spirit of Christmas while paying homage to Japan's historic warriors. His appearance during festivities is a unique cultural fusion, where the jolly, red-suited figure acquires an air of ancient dignity. This creative blend adds an intriguing dimension to the holiday celebrations, delighting children and adults alike with a distinctively Japanese take on the Christmas icon.

SANTA'S WARDROBE

1. JAPAN'S SAMURAI SANTA:

In some festivities, Santa dons a suit of armor, combining the traditional image of Saint Nick with that of a historic samurai warrior, for a unique cultural twist.

2. AUSTRALIA'S SURFING SANTA:

Ditching his usual suit for board shorts and a tank top, Santa hits the waves to celebrate Christmas Down Under, often seen with a surfboard in tow.

3. BRAZIL'S PAPAI NOEL IN LIGHTWEIGHT LINEN:

To cope with the heat, Brazil's Santa wears lighter, breathable linen, often seen in a red and white outfit that's both festive and suited to the tropical climate.

4. NETHERLANDS' SINTERKLAAS WITH A BISHOP'S MITRE:

Here, Santa looks more like a bishop, wearing traditional clerical garb complete with a tall, pointed mitre and a crosier in hand.

5. RUSSIA'S DED MOROZ WITH A MAGICAL STAFF:

Known as Grandfather Frost, he wears a long, fur-trimmed blue or red coat and carries a magical staff, symbolizing the winter season.

6. ITALY'S LA BEFANA IN A WITCH'S CLOAK:

Although not Santa, this gift-giving witch flies on a broom and wears a shawl and patched dress, delivering goodies on Epiphany Eve.

7. SWEDEN'S TOMTE, A YULE GOAT HERDER:

Santa here looks like a gnome or herder, wearing a red cap and clogs, sometimes seen with a goat, harking back to pagan Yule traditions.

8. HAWAII'S ALOHA SANTA:

Sporting a bright red Hawaiian shirt, shorts, and sometimes even flip-flops, Santa embodies the island spirit while delivering presents.

9. CHINA'S SHENGDAN LAOREN WITH A MAO CAP:

Santa merges with local culture, occasionally wearing a Mao cap instead of his traditional hat, reflecting a blend of East and West.

10. FINLAND'S JOULUPUKKI IN NORDIC STYLE:

Santa, resembling a goat named Joulupukki, wears deep red robes lined with white fur, showcasing a look that's both traditional and Nordic.

11. GREENLAND'S SEAL-SKIN SANTA:

With temperatures below freezing, Santa is often depicted in cozy, thick seal skin to keep warm during the Christmas celebrations.

12. ICELAND'S JOLASVEINAR IN WOOLEN SWEATERS:

The Yule Lads, Iceland's version of Santa, sport traditional Icelandic woolen sweaters as they bring gifts to children.

13. FRANCE'S PÈRE NOËL IN A CLOAK OF STARS:

Sometimes, Santa's outfit is adorned with stars and lights, reflecting the night sky of the Christmas season in France.

14. UNITED KINGDOM'S FATHER CHRISTMAS IN ROBES OF GREEN:

Historically, Father Christmas wore a long green, fur-lined robe, representing the coming spring and holly's evergreen nature.

15. CANADA'S MOUNTIE SANTA:

In some parades, Santa has been spotted wearing the iconic red serge of the Royal Canadian Mounted Police, honoring the national symbol.

16. GERMAN'S WEIHNACHTSMANN WITH A LANTERN:

Often depicted with a lantern to light the way, the German Santa combines elements of the old world with the traditional red coat.

17. SOUTH AFRICAN SANTA IN SAFARI GEAR:

With the holiday falling during summer, Santa might be seen in safari gear, ready to traverse the African savannah.

18. SPANISH PAPA NOEL WITH ROYAL CAPE:

Santa in Spain sometimes has a regal twist, donning a luxurious red cape fit for a king, complete with intricate embroidery.

19. NORWEGIAN JULENISSEN IN KNITTED MITTENS:

In Norway, Santa, or Julenissen, keeps cozy with hand-knitted mittens, often decorated with traditional Nordic patterns.

20. AUSTRIAN KRAMPUS IN GOAT PELTS:

Accompanying Saint Nicholas, Krampus wears dark, rustic goat pelts, contrasting Santa's bright reds with a more ominous look.

21. NEW ZEALAND'S KIWI SANTA WITH SHORTS AND GUMBOOTS:

A pragmatic choice for the summer heat, Santa's outfit includes shorts and gumboots, perfect for a Christmas on the beach.

22. GREEK AGIOS VASILIS IN A BYZANTINE ROBE:

Reflecting Orthodox traditions, the Greek version of Santa wears a robe that echoes the attire of Byzantine priests.

23. MONGOLIAN SANTA IN DEL:

In Mongolia, Santa might be seen wearing a 'del,' a traditional coat-like garment, patterned with bright colors and fur trimmings.

24. INDIAN SANTA IN A TURBAN:

Embracing local attire, Santa in India might swap his hat for a festive turban, often red and adorned with a sparkling brooch.

25. CHILEAN VIEJO PASCUERO IN PONCHO AND CHUPALLA:

In Chile, Santa, known as Viejo Pascuero, sometimes wears a poncho and a chupalla (a traditional hat), suiting the local customs and climate.

DID YOU KNOW?

In the shadow of Mount Vesuvius, Neapolitans craft a unique nativity tableau, where the manger scene unfolds against the imposing visage of the active volcano. This striking fusion symbolizes rebirth, juxtaposing the serene nativity with the volcano's potent energy. The tradition reflects the resilience of the local spirit, embracing the beauty of creation alongside the ever-present potential for destruction, and instilling a sense of awe and reflection in the Christmas celebrations of this historic Italian city.

NATIVITY NARRATIVES

1. **ITALY'S MOUNT VESUVIUS NATIVITY:**

   In Naples, a nativity scene is set with the backdrop of the active Mount Vesuvius, intertwining the story of Jesus' birth with the powerful symbol of the volcano.

2. **MEXICO'S RADISH NATIVITY:**

   Oaxaca hosts 'Noche de los Rábanos' where artisans carve intricate nativity scenes from radishes, showcasing agricultural pride with a Christmas twist.

3. **SPANISH UNDERWATER NATIVITY:**

   In certain coastal towns, divers set up underwater nativities in the sea, offering a submerged experience of the traditional Christmas story.

4. **ICELAND'S LAVA CAVE NATIVITY:**

   In a lava cave in Iceland, a nativity scene is displayed, capturing the raw beauty of nature and the warmth of the Christmas tale amidst the cold.

5. GERMAN MINIATURE NATIVITY:

In Germany, some regions create miniature nativity scenes so detailed they include tiny working mills and streams, reflecting local craftsmanship.

6. BELGIAN BEER BOTTLE NATIVITY:

Belgians have been known to construct nativity scenes entirely out of beer bottles, a nod to the country's renowned brewing tradition.

7. CANADIAN CANOE NATIVITY:

In some Canadian communities, a canoe serves as the setting for the nativity, representing the importance of this vessel in local history and culture.

8. CZECH CRYSTAL NATIVITY:

Renowned for crystal and glass craftsmanship, some Czech nativists create entire nativity scenes out of sparkling crystal.

9. NETHERLANDS' CHEESE NATIVITY:

Dutch cheese shops might display a nativity scene where all figures are carved from cheese, celebrating both the holiday and the country's famous dairy produce.

10. GUATEMALAN SAWDUST NATIVITY:

Elaborate nativity scenes are made using colored sawdust, creating vibrant and ephemeral artworks that combine religious devotion with local artistic traditions.

11. JAPANESE ORIGAMI NATIVITY:

In Japan, intricate nativities are crafted from origami, showcasing the delicate art of paper folding with a Christmas narrative.

12. KENYAN BANANA FIBER NATIVITY:

Artisans in Kenya use banana fiber to create nativity scenes, reflecting the sustainable use of local materials in Christmas celebrations.

13. NORWEGIAN GINGERBREAD NATIVITY:

Norwegians build nativity scenes from gingerbread, covering them with candies and icing, making the Christmas story both visual and edible.

14. BRAZILIAN SAND NATIVITY:

On Brazilian beaches, artists sculpt large-scale nativities from sand, drawing crowds to admire the seasonal beachfront art.

15. AUSTRIAN ICE NATIVITY:

In Austria, some sculptors carve the nativity scene out of ice, creating a glittering, frosty tableau that fits the winter landscape.

16. AMERICAN JUNKYARD NATIVITY:

In the spirit of recycling, some American communities build nativity scenes from scrap metal and car parts, turning junkyards into scenes of wonder.

17. SWISS ALPINE NATIVITY:

High in the Swiss Alps, some villages place their nativity scenes against the majestic backdrop of snow-covered mountains, blending tradition with breathtaking nature.

18. BRITISH KNITTED NATIVITY:

In the UK, knitting enthusiasts create entire nativity scenes with yarn, featuring hand-knitted figures and animals.

19. FRENCH BOULANGERIE NATIVITY:

French bakeries might craft a nativity scene from bread and pastries, celebrating the birth of Jesus with the aroma of freshly baked goods.

20. SOUTH AFRICAN BEADWORK NATIVITY:

Local artisans in South Africa use traditional beadwork to create colorful nativity scenes, showcasing a vibrant aspect of Zulu culture.

21. RUSSIAN MATRYOSHKA NATIVITY:

Russian crafters often create nativity scenes within Matryoshka nesting dolls, with each layer revealing more of the Christmas story.

22. INDONESIAN PUPPET NATIVITY:

Utilizing the traditional art of shadow puppets, Indonesians tell the nativity story through intricate puppetry, merging religious narrative with cultural performance.

23. EGYPTIAN COPTIC NATIVITY:

In Egypt, Coptic Christians create nativities in their churches that mirror ancient Egyptian art styles, often with a backdrop of the pyramids.

24. FILIPINO PAROL NATIVITY:

In the Philippines, the traditional star-shaped lanterns called 'parol' are used to construct the Star of Bethlehem above nativity scenes, illuminating the figures with a warm glow.

25. NEW ZEALAND POHUTUKAWA NATIVITY:

The pohutukawa, New Zealand's Christmas tree, often serves as the setting for nativity scenes, with its bright red flowers symbolizing the festive season.

DID YOU KNOW?

In the warm Hawaiian Christmas breeze, evergreens are adorned with vibrant leis, transforming the traditional Christmas tree into a Polynesian holiday spectacle. These fragrant garlands, usually bestowed as symbols of affection, now drape gracefully over the branches, infusing the air with the sweet scents of plumeria and orchids. This island twist to Yuletide celebrations merges the spirit of aloha with the season's joy, offering a unique and colorful alternative to the usual tinsel and ornaments, and casting a tropical spell over the festive season.

UNCONVENTIONAL TREES

1. **HAWAIIAN LEI TREES:**

   In Hawaii, Christmas trees are sometimes decorated with leis, the traditional garland of flowers, to give a tropical feel to the holiday season.

2. **UKRAINE'S SPIDER WEB TREES:**

   Ukrainians adorn their Christmas trees with spider web ornaments, a tradition stemming from a folk tale where spiders wove webs that turned into gold and silver strands on a poor family's tree.

3. **GERMANY'S CHRISTMAS PICKLE:**

   In a quirky German-American tradition, a pickle ornament is hidden within the Christmas tree branches, with the finder often receiving a reward or good fortune for the following year.

4. **JAPAN'S ORIGAMI DECORATIONS:**

   In Japan, families often decorate their Christmas trees with intricately folded origami animals and shapes, adding a unique and artistic touch to the holiday.

5. NORWAY'S JULEBUKK:

Norwegians sometimes decorate with a 'Julebukk', a Christmas goat made of straw, symbolizing the one who helped carry goods for the feast.

6. BRAZIL'S COTTON TREES:

Reflecting the snow-less Christmas of Brazil, some people use cotton to simulate snow on their Christmas trees, creating a wintery look despite the tropical climate.

7. NEW ZEALAND'S POHUTUKAWA:

In lieu of traditional pine trees, New Zealanders use the native Pohutukawa tree with its crimson flowers as a Christmas symbol, often decorating it similarly to the pine.

8. AUSTRALIAN SEASHELL TREES:

Australians living by the coast decorate their trees with seashells, starfish, and other ocean relics, celebrating Christmas during their summer season.

9. PHILIPPINES' LANTERN TREES:

Filipinos may adorn their Christmas trees with colorful 'parol', star-shaped lanterns, that symbolize the Star of Bethlehem.

10. ITALIAN WITCH ORNAMENTS:

In Italy, some trees are decorated with figures of La Befana, a friendly witch who delivers gifts, representing the Epiphany.

11. USA'S POPCORN GARLANDS:

A traditional American decoration is the popcorn garland, where families string popped corn to wrap around their Christmas trees.

12. CANADIAN MAPLE LEAF DECORATIONS:

Canadians incorporate maple leaves, often painted gold or silver, into their Christmas tree decorations, nodding to their national emblem.

13. ICELAND'S YULE LADS ORNAMENTS:

Some Icelandic Christmas trees are decorated with ornaments of the 13 Yule Lads, mischievous characters from Icelandic folklore who visit children during the 13 nights leading up to Christmas.

14. BRITISH TEA-THEMED TREES:

In Britain, a unique twist involves decorating trees with miniature teapots and teacup ornaments, celebrating the nation's love for tea.

15. SWEDISH STRAW ORNAMENTS:

Swedes traditionally decorate their trees with ornaments made of straw, a custom that harkens back to pre-Christian times.

16. DUTCH CLOG ORNAMENTS:

In the Netherlands, miniature versions of traditional wooden clogs might find their way onto Christmas trees as whimsical ornaments.

17. RUSSIAN MATRYOSHKA DOLLS:

Russian families may use miniature Matryoshka dolls as Christmas tree decorations, reflecting the country's folk art.

18. SOUTH AFRICAN SAFARI ORNAMENTS:

In South Africa, it's not uncommon to see Christmas trees adorned with ornaments shaped like safari animals, paying homage to the country's wildlife.

19. FRENCH GOURMET TREES:

French Christmas trees might be decorated with miniature utensils, wine bottles, and other culinary-themed ornaments, reflecting the importance of food in French culture.

20. SPANISH FLAMENCO DECORATIONS:

In Spain, some trees are decked out with Flamenco dancer ornaments and mini guitars, celebrating the nation's cultural art form.

21. KENYAN BEADWORK:

Kenyan Christmas trees often feature intricate beadwork and African fabric ornaments, showcasing the vibrant local craftsmanship.

22. CZECH FISH SCALES:

Czechs sometimes decorate their trees with fish scales inside clear baubles, symbolizing prosperity and good fortune.

UNCONVENTIONAL TREES

23. FINNISH SAUNA ELVES:

In Finland, it's common to see 'sauna elves', small elf figurines, as part of Christmas tree decorations, reflecting the traditional Finnish sauna culture.

24. AMERICAN SPORTS-THEMED TREES:

Sports fanatics in the U.S. might decorate their trees with ornaments representing their favorite sports teams or equipment.

25. POLISH GLASS BLOWN ORNAMENTS:

Poland is known for its beautifully crafted glass-blown ornaments, often in the shapes of fruits, stars, and famous Polish figures, adding a touch of elegance to the Christmas tree.

DID YOU KNOW?

In the pre-dawn hours of Caracas, a unique tradition unfolds as the streets brim with people gliding towards church on roller-skates. This Venezuelan Christmas ritual sees roads closed to vehicles, allowing families to skate in safety. The practice is so beloved that even local priests have blessed skates, and children go to sleep with laces tied to their toes, eagerly awaiting friends to tug on them as a wake-up call for Mass. It's a vibrant, community-centric celebration that adds wheels to the holiday spirit.

HOLIDAY TRANSPORT TROUBLES

1. VENEZUELA'S ROLLER-SKATING MASS:

In Caracas, it's traditional to roller-skate to early morning Christmas Mass, leading to the closure of streets to traffic, which can be quite a transport hurdle.

2. SWEDEN'S GOAT BURNING:

The town of Gävle erects a giant straw goat every Christmas, which has become a target for vandals who try to burn it down, resulting in a yearly struggle to keep it standing.

3. NORWAY'S HIDE YOUR BROOM:

Norwegians hide their brooms on Christmas Eve to prevent them from being stolen by witches and evil spirits, making the simple act of sweeping quite the task.

4. RUSSIAN TROIKA RIDES:

In Russia, Santa, known as Ded Moroz, often arrives in a 'troika', a sled pulled by three horses, through the snowy landscapes.

WEIRD CHRISTMAS TRADITIONS

5. GERMANY'S POST OFFICE FOR SANTA:

The small town of Himmelpfort receives thousands of letters for Santa each year, with the post office working overtime to ensure each letter is answered.

6. JAPAN'S KFC CHRISTMAS RUSH:

The tradition of eating KFC on Christmas is so popular in Japan that orders must be placed months in advance, creating logistical wonders for the fast-food chain.

7. NEW ZEALAND'S SANTA PARADES:

In New Zealand, Santa has been seen in a waka, a Māori canoe, instead of his traditional sleigh, reflecting the country's heritage.

8. VENEZUELA'S ROLLER-SKATING MASS:

In Caracas, it's traditional to roller-skate to early morning Christmas Mass, leading to the closure of streets to traffic, which can be quite a transport hurdle.

9. AUSTRALIA'S SURFING SANTA:

Santa Claus is sometimes spotted surfing the waves down under, ditching his sleigh for a surfboard to the amusement of beachgoers.

10. CANADIAN MAIL CARRIERS ON SKIS:

In some snowy parts of Canada, mail carriers deliver Christmas parcels on skis, making for a festive sight.

11. U.S. CHRISTMAS TREE TOSS:

Some Americans partake in the tradition of chucking Christmas trees out of their windows post-holiday, which can be a peculiar sight for passersby.

12. BRITISH PANTOMIME HORSES:

In the UK, Christmas pantomime often involves people dressed in horse costumes, which can be a humorous transportation method for 'Santa'.

13. FRENCH 'PÈRE FOUETTARD':

In France, Santa's companion Père Fouettard, who punishes bad children, is said to travel by donkey, creating a unique challenge in city streets.

14. DUTCH 'SINTERKLAAS' BY STEAMBOAT:

In the Netherlands, Sinterklaas arrives by steamboat from Spain, making for a grand and sometimes logistically complex entrance.

15. ICELAND'S YULE CAT LEGEND:

In Iceland, the giant Yule Cat is said to roam the snowy countryside. Folklore states that those who don't receive new clothes by Christmas are at risk of becoming his prey.

16. ITALIAN 'LA BEFANA' BY BROOMSTICK:

La Befana, the Italian Christmas witch, travels by broomstick to deliver gifts, often depicted stuck in chimneys or dealing with aerial traffic.

WEIRD CHRISTMAS TRADITIONS

17. U.S. NORAD SANTA TRACKER:

The NORAD Santa Tracker began due to a misprint in a newspaper ad, leading to annual 'tracking' of Santa's sleigh through the skies.

18. BRAZIL'S FLOATING TREES:

In Rio de Janeiro, Christmas trees float on barges in the lagoon, creating a logistical feat to keep them upright and shining.

19. FINNISH REINDEER PROBLEMS:

In Finland, Santa's reindeer must be trained not to wander off into the forests, which can cause quite a delay in the Christmas Eve journey.

20. MEXICAN 'POSADAS' PROCESSIONS:

In Mexico, the Christmas Posadas involve processions that reenact Mary and Joseph's search for shelter, often resulting in traffic stops for the participants.

21. SPANISH 'THREE KINGS' BY CAMEL:

In Spain, the Three Wise Men are said to arrive by camel, leading to humorous struggles as participants in parades learn to ride them.

22. UKRAINIAN 'DIDUKH':

Bringing the Didukh, a sheaf of wheat, into the home is a Ukrainian tradition that can be tricky, trying not to scatter grains everywhere.

23. ALASKAN SLED DOG DELIVERIES:

In remote parts of Alaska, Christmas gifts are sometimes delivered by sled dogs, traversing the snowy landscape.

24. GREENLAND'S KAYAK SANTA:

In Greenland, Santa has been known to arrive by kayak, navigating through icy waters to reach the children.

25. AUSTRIAN KRAMPUS RUN:

The Krampus, a horned Christmas demon, roams the streets of Austria, often resulting in chaotic chases and transportation woes for onlookers.

26. IRISH CANDLE IN THE WINDOW:

An Irish tradition includes placing a candle in the window on Christmas Eve, which can be a challenge to keep lit in the drafty, old cottages.

DID YOU KNOW?

In Australia, a quirky translation error once turned advertisements for the native "Christmas Bush" into a comical campaign, implying that an actual bush was festooned with festive ornaments. This shrub, naturally adorned with red or pink flowers during the holiday season, became an unwitting symbol of Yuletide decoration. The ads evoked images of Australians cheerfully trimming outdoor foliage with baubles and tinsel, blending traditional Christmas iconography with the unique flora of the Australian summer, creating a humorous mix-up in the process.

THE GREAT CHRISTMAS COMMS

1. **AUSTRALIAN "CHRISTMAS BUSH" CAMPAIGN:**

   Advertisements for Australia's native "Christmas Bush" plant were once mistranslated to suggest an actual bush decorated with ornaments.

2. **SWEDEN'S DONALD DUCK CHRISTMAS:**

   Every Christmas Eve, Swedes are glued to the TV watching Donald Duck cartoons, a tradition sparked by a mistaken belief that it was the ultimate American tradition.

3. **PORTUGAL'S "CONSOADA" MIX-UP:**

   Foreigners often misunderstand Portugal's "Consoada", a Christmas Eve feast, as a conservation effort due to its name, leading to amusing explanations.

4. **GERMAN "WEIHNACHTSMANN" VS. SANTA:**

   German "Weihnachtsmann" is often translated as "Christmas Man," leading to some funny images in English-language advertisements.

5. NORWAY'S "JULEBUKK" CONFUSION:

Norway's tradition of "Julebukk" or "Christmas Goat" was misinterpreted by some international media as a live goat being gifted, rather than the actual goat-shaped Christmas ornament.

6. SPANISH LOTTERY MISPRINT:

One year, a Spanish Christmas lottery advertisement accidentally printed the wrong winning number, leading to mass confusion and a few temporary millionaires.

7. ITALY'S "LA BEFANA" MARKETED AS A WITCH:

Marketing efforts outside Italy often misrepresent "La Befana", the friendly Christmas witch, as a Halloween figure, causing some hilarious confusion.

8. CANADA'S "MUMMERING" MISINTERPRETATION:

In Newfoundland, Canada, "Mummering" involves dressing in disguise and visiting neighbors, but it was once advertised as a fancy-dress competition to tourists, leading to some festive mix-ups.

9. GREEK "KALIKANTZARI" MISINTERPRETED:

The mischievous goblins from Greek folklore, "Kalikantzari", were once mistranslated in a travel brochure as "Christmas elves," leading to some bemused tourists.

10. FRENCH "PÈRE FOUETTARD" MISTAKEN IDENTITY:

France's "Père Fouettard", a companion to St. Nicholas who punishes naughty children, was once mistranslated in an ad as "Father Whipper," sparking concern rather than festivity.

11. ICELAND'S "YULE LADS" NAME CONFUSION:

Iceland's 13 "Yule Lads" have been mistranslated into various amusing English names, including "Spoon-Licker" and "Door-Slammer", causing giggles.

12. RUSSIAN DED MOROZ'S IDENTITY CRISIS:

Russia's Ded Moroz, often equated with Santa Claus, has been mistakenly advertised as a New Year's only figure in some countries.

13. NEW ZEALAND'S POHUTUKAWA MISPRONUNCIATION:

Advertisements mispronouncing New Zealand's Christmas tree, the Pohutukawa, have led to some quirky interpretations of the word.

14. WELSH "MARI LWYD" MISINTERPRETATION:

The "Mari Lwyd" wassailing tradition involves a horse's skull, which confused advertisers turned into a friendly pony, losing the original's spooky charm.

15. CHINESE CHRISTMAS APPLE TRADITION:

Due to a pun on the words for "Christmas" and "apple", fruit stores in China sell apples wrapped in colored paper as Christmas gifts, a concept often lost in translation elsewhere.

16. DUTCH "SINTERKLAAS" VS. SANTA CLAUS:

The Dutch Sinterklaas, arriving by boat from Spain, has been mistakenly advertised as Santa Claus in some international campaigns, much to the Dutch's amusement.

17. FINNISH "JOULUPUKKI" TRANSLATION ERROR:

Finland's "Joulupukki", actually a Christmas Goat figure, has been erroneously translated as Santa Claus in some promotional materials.

18. CZECH CHRISTMAS CARP TRADITION:

Foreigners are often amused by the Czech tradition of a live carp in the bathtub before Christmas, a fact that was once mistranslated as a "pet fish gift".

19. UKRAINIAN SPIDER WEB DECORATIONS:

Ukraine's tradition of decorating trees with spider webs (for good luck) was once mistakenly advertised as a "Halloween crossover" in a Western brochure.

20. BRAZILIAN "PAPAI NOEL" IN THE SUN:

Brazil's Christmas advertisements often have to clarify that their "Papai Noel" wears silk to cope with the heat, after confusing depictions of a traditional snowy Santa.

21. BELGIAN "SAINT NICHOLAS" VS. SANTA:

Belgium's Saint Nicholas, who visits twice in December, has been mixed up with Santa Claus in some poorly researched holiday campaigns.

22. SOUTH AFRICAN "CHRISTMAS BEETLES":

South Africa's shiny Christmas beetles, a festive symbol, were once humorously marketed as collectible ornaments in a mistranslation.

23. PHILIPPINES' "SIMBANG GABI" TRANSLATIONS:

The Philippines' "Simbang Gabi" or night masses before Christmas were once amusingly marketed as "Evening Parties" in a tourist pamphlet.

24. CATALAN "CAGA TIÓ" MISUNDERSTOOD:

Catalonia's "Caga Tió", a log that "poops" out gifts, was once described in a brochure as a magical tree stump, leading to unexpected holiday decor ideas.

25. VENEZUELAN ROLLER-SKATING TO MASS:

Venezuela's tradition of roller-skating to Christmas Mass has been advertised as a city-wide skate party, slightly missing the religious context.

DID YOU KNOW?

The annual festive season sparks a unique economic phenomenon; the humble partridge, immortalized by the classic carol "The Twelve Days of Christmas," becomes a hot commodity. As December dawns, partridge prices climb, reflecting their iconic status in holiday lore. This surge is partly whimsical, partly practical, as enthusiasts and investors alike seek to own a piece of Christmas tradition. The result is a distinctive yuletide trend, where the market value of these birds skyrockets, turning them into an unexpected seasonal investment.

THE ECONOMICS OF YULETIDE

1. PARTRIDGE PRICE HIKE:

The cost of a single partridge has soared due to its popularity from "The Twelve Days of Christmas", causing a quirky surge in partridge investments each December.

2. TURTLE DOVES' INSURANCE:

Insuring two turtle doves has become a unique holiday expense, as their symbol of love increases their value, leading to specialized insurance policies for the season.

3. FRENCH HEN FUTURES:

In France, the price of three French hens fluctuates with culinary demand around Christmas, making it a peculiar commodity in the holiday futures market.

4. CALLING BIRD CONTRACTS:

The cost of four calling birds necessitates a seasonal contract for bird trainers, creating a niche job market that peaks every December.

5. GOLDEN RING RUSH:

The price of gold spikes during the holiday season as demand for five golden rings contributes to the global gold rush, creating an unusual economic indicator.

6. GOOSE EGG INFLATION:

With six geese a-laying, the unexpected inflation of goose eggs around Christmas contributes to holiday meal cost variances, making it an economist's curiosity.

7. SWAN SWIMMING FEES:

Seven swans a-swimming require renting a pond, including maintenance and swan care costs, adding an odd expense to the Christmas budget.

8. MAID SERVICE MARKUP:

The eight maids a-milking now command a premium due to the rarity of the skill, resulting in a peculiar spike in labor costs.

9. DANCING LADY LICENSES:

Nine ladies dancing must be professionally licensed, leading to a surge in dance permit applications and a seasonal bureaucracy.

10. LORD'S LEAP LOGISTICS:

Ten lords a-leaping entail coordination of aristocratic schedules and appearance fees, which can become a peculiar logistical nightmare.

THE ECONOMICS OF YULETIDE

11. PIPER PIPING PERMITS:

Eleven pipers piping need public performance permits, which see a price hike during the holidays, impacting street performance economics.

12. DRUMMER DRUMMING DUES:

Twelve drummers drumming face union dues and performance rights fees, creating an unexpected line-item in holiday entertainment budgets.

13. CHRISTMAS TREE TARIFFS:

Import tariffs on Christmas trees can add an odd cost to the festive season, especially for rare species, affecting international holiday trade.

14. SANTA SUIT SURCHARGE:

Renting a Santa suit comes with a seasonal surcharge, reflecting the demand-driven economy of Christmas costumes.

15. WRAPPING PAPER TAX:

Wrapping paper is subject to a luxury tax in some countries, making it an unusual economic factor in gift-giving traditions.

16. EGGNOG EXCISE:

Specialty holiday drinks like eggnog are sometimes taxed at a higher rate, leading to spirited economic debates.

17. MISTLETOE MONOPOLY:

The control of mistletoe supply by few farmers creates a holiday monopoly, with prices peaking for a kiss under the Christmas plant.

18. CANDY CANE CURRENCY:

Candy canes become a form of currency in some schools and offices, creating a sweet underground economy.

19. YULE LOG LICENSING:

Broadcasting yule logs on television channels requires licensing, making it a warm but costly tradition for networks.

20. HOLIDAY BONUS BIDDING:

Year-end bonuses become a competitive market, with companies bidding for the best talents with the promise of a festive financial boost.

21. ADVENT CALENDAR ARBITRAGE:

The variety of advent calendars creates an arbitrage opportunity, with savvy shoppers profiting from the price differences.

22. CHRISTMAS MARKET MARGINS:

Stallholders at Christmas markets face high pitch fees, reflecting the premium of seasonal retail space and affecting product pricing.

23. POINSETTIA PLANT PATENTS:

Unique varieties of poinsettias are patented, leading to royalty fees that contribute to the cost of these popular Christmas plants.

24. GIFT RETURN RATE:

Post-Christmas, the gift return rate spikes, creating a seasonal economy of refunds and exchanges that retailers must account for.

25. CHRISTMAS LIGHT LEVY:

Some localities charge a 'light levy' for extravagant Christmas light displays to cover the increased use of public services, adding a twinkling twist to municipal economics.

DID YOU KNOW?

In Greenland, a unique law dictates that Santas cannot demand payment for their festive appearances. This has led to the comical yet poignant spectacle of Santas on strike, brandishing signs and humorously campaigning for their right to receive at least a Christmas cookie as a token of appreciation for their jolly services. Their protests serve as a whimsical reminder of the season's spirit, where even in the far north, the value of Santa's cheer is beyond monetary measure.

YULE LAWS AND LEGISLATION

1. SANTAS ON STRIKE:

In Greenland, it's illegal for Santas to charge for their appearances, leading to the humorous image of Santas picketing for their right to earn a Christmas cookie.

2. SILENT NIGHT, LEGAL NIGHT:

Austria enforces a law requiring all residents to maintain a "quiet night" on December 24th, making even the slightest jingle bell a legal matter.

3. MINCE PIE BAN:

Oliver Cromwell briefly outlawed mince pies in England during the 17th century, a law that was never officially repealed, leaving Brits in a deliciously rebellious state each Christmas.

4. DECORATION DURATION:

In Maine, it's a punishable offense to have Christmas decorations up after January 14th, ensuring the town doesn't look like a year-round winter wonderland.

5. ILLEGAL YULE LOGS:

In a bizarre twist, an old law in England forbids the burning of Yule logs on any day other than Christmas, a law largely ignored today.

6. FORBIDDEN FESTIVITIES:

Until the late 20th century, Albania had a law strictly prohibiting the celebration of Christmas, turning any festive cheer into an act of defiance.

7. SANTA'S WEIGHT CLAUSE:

In the Australian town of Warrnambool, any mall Santa exceeding 140 kg must have a second chair for support, making Santa's belly a legal issue.

8. REINDEER RIGHTS:

In Alaska, it's illegal to give alcoholic beverages to a moose, which includes Santa's reindeer should they decide to stop over during their Christmas Eve journey.

9. MANDATORY MERRIMENT:

In Peru, there's a law requiring citizens to spend Christmas Day visiting friends, turning socializing into a legal obligation.

10. CANDY CANE CODE:

A small town in Georgia has an ordinance that candy canes must be striped with red and white, making non-conforming candy canes contraband.

11. CHRISTMAS TREE TAXES:

In some U.S. states, Christmas trees are taxed like regular goods, but in others, they're considered agricultural products and are tax-exempt, leading to a holly, jolly tax confusion.

12. GIFT WRAPPING REGULATIONS:

France has a decree that all gift wrapping paper must be recyclable, adding an eco-friendly twist to the unwrapping frenzy.

13. CAROL COPYRIGHTS:

In certain countries, singing Christmas carols in public without paying royalties is a no-go, making caroling a potential legal minefield.

14. BAN ON BELLS:

A small town in Germany prohibits the ringing of church bells at midnight on Christmas Eve to prevent noise pollution, dampening the traditional clamor.

15. LIGHTS OUT LAW:

Some areas in California restrict the hours Christmas lights can be on, to reduce light pollution and energy use, bringing a literal meaning to "all is calm."

16. CHRISTMAS DAY WORK BAN:

In Massachusetts, it's illegal for certain businesses to open on Christmas, ensuring workers can stay home, with hefty fines for non-compliance.

17. ANTI-SANTA CLAUSE:

A law in South Carolina prohibits over 30 Santas from gathering at once, to prevent confusion among children (and traffic congestion).

18. ELF EMPLOYMENT ACT:

In Iceland, any portrayal of elves must be done respectfully, due to their cultural significance, putting a legal shield around these mythical helpers.

19. NOISY TOY BAN:

In parts of Europe, toys that exceed a certain noise level cannot be sold during the Christmas season, keeping peace and quiet under the tree.

20. PUDDING PROTECTION:

In the UK, Christmas pudding recipes are safeguarded by law, ensuring that traditional methods and ingredients are used, protecting the heritage of the holiday dessert.

21. CHRISTMAS BONUS MANDATE:

In Mexico, employers are legally required to pay a Christmas bonus, called "aguinaldo," ensuring everyone gets a little extra holiday cheer.

22. ORNAMENT ORDINANCE:

A town in Vermont has a quirky law that all Christmas ornaments must be made of biodegradable material, making for a very green Christmas.

23. NO KRIS KRINGLE KISSING:

In Indiana, it's reportedly illegal for a man with a mustache to "habitually kiss human beings," a rule that impacts many a whiskered Santa.

24. TINSEL TAX:

In an odd twist of legislation, some U.S. states classify tinsel as a "luxury item," thereby subjecting it to higher taxes during the festive season.

25. HOLIDAY MUSIC LIMIT:

A law in the Philippines limits the playing of Christmas music in public places to within the 'Ber' months (September-December), preserving the specialness of holiday tunes.

DID YOU KNOW?

In the sun-soaked yards of Florida, a playful holiday tradition takes flight with vibrant flocks of plastic flamingos donning jolly Santa hats. These cheerful charades materialize overnight, much to the bemusement of homeowners. This whimsical practice, known locally as "flocking," embodies the lighthearted spirit of the season. The fake birds, often arranged in comical scenarios, serve not only as a prank among friends but also as a quirky symbol of Floridian Christmas cheer, merging tropical vibes with festive merriment.

POLAR PRANKS

1. **FESTIVE FAKE FLAMINGOS:**

   In Florida, flocks of plastic flamingos wearing Santa hats may mysteriously appear in your yard, a whimsical prank that's become a local holiday tradition.

2. **INVISIBLE MISTLETOE:**

   In Sweden, it's a cheeky tradition to hang an 'invisible mistletoe' and watch as people awkwardly contemplate following the kissing tradition with nothing overhead.

3. **GIFT-WRAPPED ROOMS:**

   In Australia, friends often wrap everything in a buddy's room, from the bed to individual pens, in festive paper for a Christmas surprise.

4. **SNEAKY SNOWMEN:**

   In Japan, it's common to create snowmen with a surprise water balloon core, so when kids go to demolish them, they end up in a splash!

5. **CHRISTMAS TREE SWITCHEROO:**

   In Canada, pranksters secretly swap a neighbor's decorated Christmas tree with an undecorated one, leaving them bewildered on Christmas morning.

6. ICY HOT CHOCOLATE:

In Russia, it's a playful trick to serve hot chocolate cubes that are actually frozen, leading to confused sips and laughs all around.

7. BOGUS PRESENT BRICKS:

In Ireland, it's common to wrap up bricks and put them under the tree as fake heavy gifts, adding a literal 'weight' to the anticipation.

8. CHIMNEY CAMOUFLAGE:

In Italy, some jokesters will cover the chimney entrance with cling film, creating a sticky trap for any 'Santa' trying to come down.

9. CHRISTMAS CAROL CHAOS:

In the UK, pranksters might sing altered lyrics to classic carols door-to-door, resulting in giggles or confused expressions from the audience.

10. FAKE SNOW FOOTPRINTS:

In New Zealand, fake snow footprints leading out of the house are used to convince kids that Santa accidentally walked the wrong way.

11. REINDEER ROAMING ALERTS:

In the U.S., parents might set up 'reindeer cams' and create faux alerts on their phones to show kids evidence of reindeer in the area.

12. PUDDING PUZZLES:

In South Africa, a humorous trick is to hide a tiny puzzle piece in the Christmas pudding, ensuring a perplexed eater – and a promise of more dessert once the puzzle is solved.

13. ELF ON THE SHELF MISCHIEFS:

Across many countries, parents position the 'Elf on the Shelf' in naughty scenarios, like making a mess with flour or unwrapping presents.

14. UNTIE-ABLE BOWS:

In France, it's a funny prank to tie bows on gifts with a special knot that's almost impossible to open by hand.

15. JINGLE BELL JOKES:

In Mexico, pranksters attach jingle bells to doors and windows, so every entrance and exit becomes a noisy announcement.

16. SANTA'S 'CRASH LANDING':

In Brazil, some create a mock scene of Santa's sleigh 'crashing' into their yard, complete with scattered presents and reindeer tracks.

17. CONFETTI CRACKERS:

In the Netherlands, Christmas crackers are sneakily filled with confetti, so when pulled, they shower the room and guests with a festive explosion.

WEIRD CHRISTMAS TRADITIONS

18. MISMATCHED SHOES:

In Finland, a funny Christmas morning prank involves mixing up all the shoes in the house, causing a comical search for the right pair.

19. FLOATING DECORATIONS:

In the Philippines, it's not uncommon to find Christmas decorations hung with clear thread across pathways, causing a startle when people walk into seemingly floating objects.

20. CANDY COAL:

In Spain, pranksters replace one sweet in a box of chocolates with a piece of edible 'coal', an unexpected bite for the unsuspecting.

21. UPSIDE-DOWN TREE:

In Poland, a playful trick is to mount the Christmas tree upside down from the ceiling, creating a topsy-turvy holiday scene.

22. CAROLING FLASH MOB:

In the USA, groups might surprise a friend by showing up unannounced and performing an over-the-top carol performance in their front yard.

23. DESSERT DECEPTION:

In Belgium, bakers might create a dessert that looks savory, like a pie that's actually made of sweet marzipan and fruit.

24. WHOOPEE CUSHION CAROLS:

In Germany, it's a jocular prank to hide whoopee cushions on seats before a Christmas concert, causing a symphony of unexpected 'notes'.

25. WRAPPED DOORWAYS:

In Denmark, pranksters carefully wrap doorways in festive paper, so when people try to walk through, they get a face-full of Christmas cheer.

DID YOU KNOW?

In Sweden, a playful twist on the mistletoe tradition involves using lingonberry branches, a common Scandinavian shrub. During the festive season, these branches are playfully hung in homes as if they were mistletoe. Unsuspecting guests often find themselves standing beneath these impostor sprigs, prompting a mix of bewilderment and amusement when they're informed of the custom and encouraged to partake in a kiss, adding a uniquely Swedish humorous touch to the universal tradition of holiday affection.

MISTLETOE MISHAPS

1. SWEDEN'S LINGONBERRY TWIST:

Swedes sometimes use lingonberry branches as a stand-in for mistletoe, leading to confused looks and laughter when visitors are told they're standing under a 'kissing plant'.

2. CANADA'S MAPLE MISTLETOE:

In a humorous nod to their heritage, some Canadians hang maple leaves instead of mistletoe and insist it has the same power, prompting unexpected smooches.

3. FRENCH TRIPLE KISS:

In France, it's common to kiss on both cheeks, but under the mistletoe, an extra kiss is required, leading to amusing encounters.

4. GERMAN MISTLETOE MIX-UP:

Germans have a tradition of a 'kissing sprig', and sometimes a leafless branch is hung by pranksters, prompting jokes about 'kissing on a budget'.

5. SCOTTISH THISTLE UNDERFOOT:

As a joke, Scots sometimes place a thistle under the mistletoe, making the kiss brave effort as they try to avoid the prickles.

6. AUSTRALIAN SURFBOARD SURPRISE:

Australians at beach parties may hang mistletoe over a surfboard propped in the sand, catching sunbathers off-guard for a sandy smooch.

7. ICELAND'S VOLCANIC MISTLETOE:

Playing on Iceland's volcanic landscape, a piece of lava rock is sometimes hung, teasing that kisses will be as hot as lava.

8. ITALIAN BISCOTTO BLUNDER:

In Italy, a biscotto (cookie) is sometimes jokingly used instead of mistletoe, leading to laughter when someone tries to eat the 'kissing token'.

9. RUSSIAN DOLL DILEMMA:

Russians sometimes hide mistletoe in Matryoshka dolls, and the person who opens the last one is owed kisses from the group, sparking chuckles and a dash for the doll.

10. JAPANESE PAPER MISTLETOE:

In Japan, origami mistletoe is a cute twist, but it sometimes leads to awkward moments when it's mistaken for just another paper decoration.

11. DUTCH CLOG CONFUSION:

In the Netherlands, mistletoe is occasionally replaced with a pair of miniature clogs, leaving guests wondering if they should kiss or just admire the shoes.

12. BRAZILIAN CARNIVAL MISTLETOE:

Brazilians might use a colorful feather boa in place of mistletoe during Christmas, blending Carnival spirit into the holiday festivities.

13. BELGIAN CHOCOLATE MISTLETOE:

A Belgian prank involves hanging chocolate shaped like mistletoe, leading to sweet surprises instead of kisses.

14. AMERICAN FLASH MOB KISS:

In the U.S., flash mobs sometimes form under large mistletoe installations in malls, leading to mass-kissing spectacles and lots of giggles.

15. SPANISH FLAMENCO FLUB:

In Spain, some hang mistletoe on a flamenco dancer's dress as a joke, prompting a passionate dance before a peck.

16. GREEK OLIVE BRANCH OFFER:

Greeks, known for their olive trees, might use an olive branch as mistletoe, causing confusion but also symbolizing peace before the peck.

17. TURKISH DELIGHT TRICK:

In Turkey, a piece of Turkish delight is sometimes hung where mistletoe should be, leading to laughs when someone tries to take a bite.

18. SOUTH AFRICAN SAFARI SPIN:

South Africans might place mistletoe on safari vehicles, causing chuckles when tourists find themselves obligated to kiss amidst the wild.

19. ENGLISH TEA-TIME TANGLE:

In England, it's a cheeky custom to hang mistletoe over the teapot during tea time, causing a stir when guests reach for a refill.

20. INDIAN GARLAND GAFFE:

In India, garlands are sometimes mischievously hung in place of mistletoe, leading to a festive, but confused, embrace.

21. IRISH CLOVER CONFUSION:

The Irish might replace mistletoe with a four-leaf clover string, giving a lucky twist to the kissing game.

22. POLISH PIEROGI PLOY:

A playful tradition in Poland involves hanging a pierogi dumpling instead of mistletoe, leading to laughter when someone reaches for a kiss and gets a dumpling instead.

23. NORWEGIAN SKI SLIP:

In Norway, mistletoe is hung over ski racks, and the slippery encounter when skiers, clad in gear, try to exchange kisses is a source of amusement.

24. FILIPINO STAR LANTERN SWAP:

Filipinos hang their traditional star lanterns, or parols, in place of mistletoe, creating a starry-eyed kissing scene.

25. NEW ZEALAND KIWI QUIRK:

New Zealanders sometimes use a kiwi fruit vine instead of mistletoe, causing a humorous hesitation as people debate whether a kiss or a kiwi is coming their way.

DID YOU KNOW?

In Norway, Santas engage in a whimsical form of training known as Chimney Gymnastics, where they master the skill of gracefully navigating narrow spaces. They practice on a range of mock chimneys, each with different circumferences, to hone their mythical descent. This training ensures that every Santa can slide down chimneys of all sizes with elegance and dexterity, keeping the enchanting illusion of Santa's entry intact for awe-inspired children who eagerly anticipate the magical appearance of their Christmas gifts.

SANTA SCHOOL

1. **CHIMNEY GYMNASTICS:**

   In Norway, Santas are taught the art of entering tight spaces with grace, often practicing in mock chimneys with varying girths to perfect their mythical descent technique.

2. **REINDEER ETIQUETTE:**

   Canadian Santa schools include reindeer communication classes, where Santas learn the basics of reindeer body language to ensure smooth sleigh rides on Christmas Eve.

3. **ELF MANAGEMENT 101:**

   In the U.S., Santa trainees attend workshops on managing the diverse personalities of elves to keep toy production efficient and harmonious.

4. **PANTOMIME PARCEL PLACEMENT:**

   UK Santa academies focus on silent present delivery, mastering the art of tiptoeing and gesture to avoid waking sleeping children and pets.

5. **ROOFTOP READINESS:**

   In Switzerland, Santas practice navigating steep rooftops with mock sleighs to ensure no chimney is unreachable, regardless of the snow depth.

6. SLEIGH MECHANIC SKILLS:

In Germany, Santa students learn the intricacies of sleigh maintenance, from runners to magical propulsion systems, to prevent mid-air breakdowns.

7. HO-HO-HO VOCAL TRAINING:

Australian Santa schools employ voice coaches to help Santas develop a belly laugh that's jolly yet soothing, perfect for any Christmas occasion.

8. COOKIE CONNOISSEUR CLASSES:

In Belgium, future Santas are educated in the fine art of cookie tasting, learning to discern between dozens of holiday treats without gaining a pound.

9. BEARD GROOMING:

Japanese Santa courses include beard care, where Santas learn how to maintain a fluffy, white beard that resists cookies crumbs and milk dribbles.

10. GIFT WRAPPING GYMNASTICS:

In Brazil, Santas are trained in the high-speed wrapping of oddly shaped gifts, ensuring no present is too challenging to disguise.

11. NAUGHTY OR NICE NEGOTIATIONS:

French Santas attend seminars on psychology to better understand the gray areas between 'naughty' and 'nice' in children's behavior.

12. EXPRESS EMOTION EYEBROWS:

Russian Santa schools teach the art of expressive eyebrows, enabling Santas to convey warmth and kindness without saying a word.

13. MULTI-LINGUAL MERRIMENT:

In South Africa, Santas learn key phrases in multiple languages to deliver personalized greetings to children from diverse backgrounds.

14. MISTLETOE DIPLOMACY:

Finnish Santa training includes conflict resolution under the mistletoe, ensuring peace and joy reign supreme during family gatherings.

15. SANTA SURVIVAL SKILLS:

In Alaska, Santa training includes survival skills for the North Pole's harsh conditions, from igloo building to emergency present repairs.

16. SOOT STAIN REMOVAL:

Italian Santas are well-versed in the quick removal of soot stains from their suits, using magic and a bit of elbow grease.

17. LIST LOGISTICS:

In the Netherlands, there's a focus on list management, teaching Santas the most efficient ways to double-check who's been naughty or nice.

18. JINGLE BELL JAZZERCISE:

In the U.S., Santas engage in dance classes to ensure they can ho-ho-ho in rhythm to any Christmas tune.

19. SLEIGH PARKING PRECISION:

In Monaco, precision parking of the sleigh is practiced, as Santas must navigate the tiny principality's luxurious and crowded rooftops.

20. HIGH-TECH TOY TROUBLESHOOTING:

In South Korea, Santas are trained in the latest toy technology, ensuring they can operate and fix any gadget on the spot.

21. SEASONAL SIGN LANGUAGE:

In international Santa schools, sign language is taught so Santas can communicate with all children, making no child feels left out.

22. FESTIVE FIRST AID:

In Denmark, Santas are trained in first aid to ensure they can handle any Christmas emergency, from paper cuts to pudding overindulgence.

23. HOLIDAY HISTORY:

In Greece, Santas delve into the rich history of St. Nicholas, learning to recount his stories and traditions with accuracy and spirit.

24. WEATHER FORECASTING FOR SLEIGHING:

In Argentina, Santas study weather patterns to plan the safest and most efficient routes for delivering presents.

25. CHARITABLE CHEER SPREADING:

In India, Santa training includes lessons on spreading cheer beyond presents, teaching Santas to leave a lasting impact through acts of kindness and community service.

DID YOU KNOW?

In the depths of Germany's festive traditions lies the whimsical "German Gherkin Game." A glass ornament shaped like a green pickle is clandestinely nestled among the dense pine needles of the family Christmas tree. Shrouded in the tree's festive attire, it awaits the keen eyes of children on Christmas morning. The first to discover the hidden gherkin is rewarded not only with a specially reserved extra present but also the promise of a year's worth of good luck, a delightful incentive that adds to the magic of the holiday season.

THE CHRISTMAS PICKLE

1. GERMAN GHERKIN GAMES:

A pickle ornament is stealthily placed within the boughs of the Christmas tree. The first child to spot it on Christmas morning receives an extra gift and good fortune for the coming year.

2. AMERICAN PICKLE PRIZES:

In the U.S., finding the Christmas pickle might win you a special prize or the privilege of opening the first present, adding a competitive edge to the holiday cheer.

3. SPANISH SURPRISE:

Spain has adopted the pickle tradition with a twist; finding it can mean you'll be the one to serve or clean up after the Christmas feast.

4. CANADIAN SWEET PICKLE:

Some Canadians have a sweeter take, hiding a candy cane pickle and rewarding the finder with a jar of real pickles or a sweet treat.

5. MEXICAN EL PEPINILLO PARTY:

In Mexico, some celebrate finding the pickle with a mini fiesta or a special dance around the Christmas tree.

6. ITALIAN PICKLED PROVERB:

Italians who partake say "Chi trova il sottaceto trova il tesoro" meaning "He who finds the pickle, finds the treasure," rewarding the finder with a small treasure chest.

7. FRENCH 'CORNICHON CACHÉ':

The French 'hidden gherkin' is a relatively new concept, and finding it means you'll have a year of wisdom ahead.

8. BRAZILIAN 'PICLES DA SORTE':

Brazilians call it the "Pickle of Luck," and it's said to bring a year of good health to whoever discovers it.

9. AUSTRALIAN ANTIPODEAN PICKLE:

Aussies have turned it upside down, often hanging the pickle at the bottom of the tree, making it harder to find in the Southern Hemisphere.

10. SWEDISH 'INLAGD GURKA':

In Sweden, finding the pickled cucumber decoration means you get an extra helping of the traditional Christmas porridge.

THE CHRISTMAS PICKLE

11. DUTCH 'AUGURKJE VINDEN':

The Dutch version involves a quirky poem that's read out before the tree is searched, and the finder is granted the honor of reading the Christmas story.

12. RUSSIAN 'OGURETS OTKRYTIE':

The Russian tradition includes hiding a pickle and the finder gets to hide it the next year, ensuring a cycle of pickle-themed fun.

13. JAPANESE 'KUKKĪ NO TSUKEMONO':

In Japan, the concept is often tied to a New Year's tradition, with the pickle finder receiving a blessing from the elders.

14. SOUTH AFRICAN 'KERFEES KOMKOMMER':

South Africans who adopt this tradition might also include a small gift alongside the pickle as a symbol of generosity.

15. BELGIAN 'PICKLE POEM':

Belgians who follow the tradition write a special poem about the pickle and the person who finds it must recite it.

16. AUSTRIAN 'GURKEN GLÜCK':

For Austrians who observe this, the pickle is often made of delicate glass and finding it is a sign of resilience for the upcoming year.

17. NORWEGIAN 'JULEAGURK':

In Norway, children who find the pickle are often tasked with handing out the Christmas presents to everyone else.

18. ICELANDIC 'GÚRKUR LEIKUR':

The Icelandic game involves not just finding the pickle but also performing a traditional dance or song as a show of festive spirit.

19. POLISH 'OGÓREK OZDOBA':

In Poland, the pickle ornament is often accompanied by other food-themed decorations, and the finder gets to choose the Christmas dessert.

20. CZECH 'OKURKA OBJEV':

In the Czech Republic, finding the pickle means you've been the most observant throughout the year, a trait praised among friends and family.

21. FINNISH 'PIKKELI PIILOSSA':

Finns might hide a real pickle among the branches, and the finder has to eat it before presents can be opened.

22. TURKISH 'TURŞU TAPMAK':

Although not a traditional practice, some in Turkey have adopted the pickle hunt, and finding it means you'll be the toast of the Christmas table.

23. NEW ZEALAND 'PICKLE PROWESS':

In New Zealand, finding the pickle might also mean you get to place the star or angel atop the tree.

24. INDIAN 'ACHAAR KI KHOJ':

In India, those who celebrate Christmas might incorporate the pickle tradition with a local twist, hiding a mango pickle and giving a small gift to the finder.

25. GREEK 'POLICHRONO PIKELIA':

Greeks who practice the pickle tradition may have it symbolize the many years of life, with the finder expected to live the longest and healthiest life.

DID YOU KNOW?

Amidst the vast, starry expanse of space, astronauts aboard the International Space Station indulge in celestial holiday spirit by crafting makeshift ornaments to adorn their high-tech home. Utilizing materials at hand, such as reflective tin foil, colorful wires, and bits of cloth, they create glimmering decorations that float in zero gravity. These festive creations bring a touch of Earth's Christmas cheer to the compact, utilitarian quarters of the space station, transforming the orbiting laboratory into a cosmic winter wonderland, far above the world's snowy silences.

YULETIDE IN SPACE

1. **ORBITING ORNAMENTS:**

   Astronauts have been known to decorate their spacecraft with makeshift ornaments, like using tin foil and other materials to bring festive cheer to the compact space station quarters.

2. **SPACE STOCKINGS:**

   Crew members aboard the International Space Station often hang personalized stockings by their sleeping pods, a touch of home amidst the stars.

3. **ZERO-G CAROLS:**

   Singing Christmas carols while floating in zero gravity has become a cherished tradition for astronauts, creating a unique chorus that resonates through the spacecraft.

4. **THE VELCRO FEAST:**

   Space-friendly Christmas meals are attached to tables with Velcro, featuring rehydrated delicacies to simulate traditional holiday fare.

5. ORBITAL SECRET SANTA:

Astronauts participate in a Secret Santa, exchanging small gifts that have been brought to space, often with a personal or humorous touch.

6. COSMIC CHRISTMAS TREE:

A small, artificial tree or even a tablet displaying a festive image serves as the central decoration for astronauts longing for traditional holiday visuals.

7. SANTA'S SPACE SLEIGH:

Some astronauts have donned Santa hats or full costumes, playfully claiming to spot Santa's sleigh from the cupola windows.

8. STAR-GAZING SILENT NIGHT:

Astronauts often describe spending Christmas Eve watching the Earth or the stars, reflecting on the silence and beauty of space.

9. WEIGHTLESS WRAPPING:

Gift wrapping in space is a challenge, with everything floating around, making for some creatively packaged presents.

10. SPACE STATION NATIVITY:

Figurines from a nativity scene have been brought aboard and displayed, symbolizing the global and universal nature of the holiday spirit.

11. REINDEER GAMES:

Astronauts mimic reindeer games in zero gravity, inventing new traditions and games that can only be played while floating.

12. SATELLITE SANTA TRACKING:

From the ISS, astronauts support the NORAD Santa-tracking tradition, providing "first-hand" updates on his progress around Earth.

13. GALACTIC GINGERBREAD:

Building a gingerbread space station instead of a house has become a fun way for astronauts to get creative with their holiday treats.

14. INTERSTELLAR CHRISTMAS CARDS:

Sending digital Christmas cards from space to loved ones on Earth, adorned with photos of Earth and space vistas.

15. HOLIDAY SCIENCE EXPERIMENTS:

Performing themed experiments, like observing crystallization in zero gravity to create space snowflakes.

16. SPACE SUIT STOCKINGS:

Using spare space suit gloves as stockings, astronauts fill them with small treats and trinkets.

17. FLOATING FILM FESTIVAL:

Watching classic Christmas movies on a laptop strapped to a wall, enjoying the comforts of familiar stories while orbiting Earth.

18. COSMIC COUNTDOWN:

Celebrating Christmas countdowns with the ship's systems, marking the 12 days to Christmas with a fun fact about space or the mission each day.

19. ASTRO-ADVENT CALENDAR:

Creating a digital advent calendar with a space fact or image behind each "door," opened daily.

20. STARRY NIGHT STORYTIME:

Reading Christmas stories or poems aloud, with the backdrop of the Earth or space adding to the magic of the tales.

21. JINGLE BELLS JETPACK:

Playing Christmas music over the station's communication system, with 'Jingle Bells' being a perennial favorite.

22. ALIEN ANGEL TREE TOPPER:

Jokingly topping the Christmas display with a friendly "alien" angel, celebrating the hope of peace across the universe.

23. ROCKET-FUELED REVELRY:

Sharing favorite holiday memories over the radio, connecting with family and mission control with stories of past celebrations.

24. ORBITING EARTHLIGHT:

Using the Earth's reflection as their "Christmas lights," astronauts admire the glow of cities and natural phenomena like the aurora borealis.

25. NEW YEAR'S ORBITAL OVATION:

Celebrating New Year's multiple times as they orbit the Earth, astronauts enjoy the unique perspective of welcoming the new year in many time zones.

Printed in Great Britain
by Amazon